Your Walrus Hurt The One You Love

Your Walrus Hurt The One You Love

Malapropisms, mispronunciations and linguistic cock-ups.

Philip Norman

ELM TREE BOOKS LONDON

First published in Great Britain 1985
by Elm Tree Books Ltd
Garden House 57-59 Long Acre London WC2E 9JZ

Design by Craig Dodd

Norman, Philip
  Your walrus hurts the one you love: malapropisms,
  mispronounciations and linguistic cock-ups.
  1. Malapropisms   2. English wit and humor
  I. Title
  827′.914′08   PN6231.M1/

  ISBN 0-241-11672-4

Typeset by Pioneer, East Sussex
Printed in Great Britain by
Billing and Sons Ltd, Worcester.

Contents

Introduction

When Sheridan's Mrs Malaprop irritably complained that Lydia Languish was as 'headstrong as an allegory on the banks of the Nile', she was not inventing, merely mal-appropriating the foible that bears her name. Two centuries earlier in *Much Ado About Nothing*, Dogberry the constable had proudly 'comprehended two aspicious persons' at the head of his 'dissembly'. Other figures in literature are at least the stately dame's equal at speaking *mal apropos*. In Smollett's *Humphry Clinker*, Mrs Winifred Jenkins threatens to succumb to a fit of 'asterisks'. Mincing, the maid in Congreve's *Way of the World*, announces that dinner is 'impatient'. We would speak of Dogberries, Jenkinses, Mincings (or, for that matter, Bottoms, Mistress Quicklies, even Pecksniffs or Gamps) if there were any justice in literature. But let it pass: as Dogberry observes elsewhere, 'comparisons are odorous'.

The fact is that the English are a nation of malapropists and that our language in its richest parts derives from our reluctance to pronounce any word — especially any foreign

1

word — correctly, if we can help it. The urge to malaprop arises from three fine old English qualities. The first is unrepentant ignorance. The second is contempt for other races. The third is the steadfast belief that whatever any English person says must be right. Add to

2

this our love of pun and conundrum and our deeply-ingrained embarrassment about organised religion, and you can see how 'bloody' as an oath mutated from the sacrilegious 'By Our Lady', or how a tavern named after the Infanta of Castile ended up as the Elephant and Castle.

This book owes its origin to a slow week on the *Sunday Times* Atticus column, when I casually invited readers to send in their favourite malapropism. The result kept the column going — and its editor semi-hysterical — for three consecutive weeks. The letters, ratting on grandmothers, aunts, parents, children, employers, spouses and lovers, were uniformly affectionate. Malapropists, I realise, are beloved members of society, cherished by the people they so unwittingly entertain. Part of the sublime innocence that launches them into their mid-air verbal collisions and linguistic pratfalls is never realising how many aficionados are standing by, hanging on to their every pulverised word.

Since leaving Atticus, I have gone on collecting examples from friends, colleagues and correspondents all over Britain and America. In making this selection, I have discarded mere hapless puns and concentrated on the flights of brilliant alternative imagery that distinguish the truly inspired malapropist. I happen to have the sort of mind that would rather believe that curtains hang from a 'pelvis', that men in evening dress hold their trousers up with a 'camembert' and that children in World War II were saved from the London blitz by being 'evaporated'. Not that these verbal Dalis deal only in the fantastical. Greater truth than they know may be spoken by malapropists who come to you with the 'mucus' of an idea, or describe how they 'hee'd and hawed' before buying something because the price was so 'exuberant'. An incidental joy has been to discover how little the glorious urge is a respecter of class or profession. I was recently shown a letter to a New York publisher from a high-powered literary agent, confidently vouchsafing that his client's new novel was 'jettisoned' for the best-seller list.

Where malapropisms blur into spoonerism, mixed metaphor or double entendre, I have allowed them to blur. What's the good of doing something like this if one can't be a *little* self-divulgent?

Philip Norman, New York, 1985

Grateful thanks to Peter Miln, Ned Sherrin, Tracey Norman, Ronald Mansbridge, George Brock, John Young and readers of *The Times* and *The New York Times Book Review*.

'Just a lot of belladonnas . . .'

Malapropisms of the Mighty

President Ronald Reagan's reliance on cue-cards which his contact lenses sometimes cannot fully distinguish makes him a mala-propist *par excellence*. The other month he demonstrated the fact yet again at a White House reception by introducing President Samuel Doe of Liberia to the American nation as 'Chairman Moe'. In another famous speech, grasping for a Biblical allusion to support nuclear proliferation, the President attempted to say 'Samson slew the Philistines' but actually said 'Simpson slew the Philippines'.

The late Lord Drogheda, when chairman of the *Financial Times*, coined a fine double-header in describing the mix-up over two paintings in a friend's ancestral home. What had been thought to be a Tintoretto proved on examination to be a Canaletto. 'They thought it was a Rio Tinto,' his Lordship explained. 'Now they've discovered it's a Rigoletto.'

During the visit of President John F. Kennedy and his fashionable young wife to Paris in 1962, a new word became the vogue among the White House press corps — 'treasurely'. Everything in Paris, the correspondents told one another, was 'just too treasurely'.

The word is said to have derived from Jackie Kennedy's remark on visiting the Louvre and seeing the Mona Lisa:

'Oh — it's très jolie.'

John Lennon was as much a malapropist by accident as a punster by design. George Martin, the Beatles' record producer, remembers taking Lennon to dinner in a restaurant when he was first down from Liverpool. A waiter approached with a dish and murmured *'Mange-tout*, Sir?' 'Okay,' Lennon agreed cautiously, 'but put 'em over there, not anywhere near the food.'

An earnest BBC interviewer once asked Lennon if in his writing he made 'conscious use of onomatopoeia'.

'I dunno what that feller was on about,' Lennon said later. 'He kept on talking about an automatic pier.'

Lord Blyton, the 84-year-old former MP for Durham, was asked by a journalist how he rated his fellow peers' performance in the first televised Lords debate.

'Waste of time,' he muttered. 'They're all just a lot of belladonnas.'

America's most renowned civic malapropist was the terrible Mayor Richard Daley of Chicago. In 1968, after Daley's police had run amok through the Democratic party convention, the Mayor appeared on television to refute charges of unnecessary violence. 'I'll say just one thing on this,' Daley began in his accustomed Irish bellow. 'It's the police's job to preserve disorder. And they *preserved* disorder . . .'

On a lighter occasion, the Mayor was invited to endorse the riding of tandems as a way of promoting harmony between married couples. Daley performed an unsteady circuit on the rear of a tandem, then came to the waiting microphones.

'I just wanna say,' he bellowed, 'you husbands and wives, if you wanna get along together, you gotta get one of these tantrum bicycles . . .'

An NUM official, interviewed on Radio 4 after the year-long miners' strike, angrily described the National Coal Board as 'totally incontinent'.

The Princess of Wales, opening a new hospital wing in Northamptonshire — at a time when National Health malingering was much in the news — said she hoped the new facility would be used by people 'lying in the district'.

An NUM official described the National Coal
Board as totally incontinent . . .

While running for President in 1971, Alabama's white supremist Governor George Wallace realised he must strike a chord of brotherhood with the Negro voter.

'Sure, ah look like a white man . . .' Wallace told a large assembly of his prospective brothers. 'But mah heart is as black as anybody's heah.'

The utterances of Samuel Goldwyn showed to what height the malapropism could be taken by huge Philistinism married to enormous power. 'A verbal agreement's not worth the paper it's written on' summed up the great film mogul's business ethos. A suggestion that he should show charity to a competitor, who happened to be an old friend, was dismissed by the pragmatic reflection, 'We've passed a lot of water under the bridge since then.'

At critical moments, Goldwyn was apt to warn his subordinates that MGM studios stood 'on the brink of an abscess'. Informed there was a dearth of Indian extras in a new Western epic, he brusquely ordered, 'Get some more from the reservoir.'

On a rare occasion, a new production his subordinates had praised as 'magnificent' stirred Samuel Goldwyn to the depths. 'It's more than magnificent,' he said. 'It's *mediocre*!'

In 1980, the word-strangling General Alexander Haig declined to answer a Senate Committee question on the grounds that it was 'too suppository'.

A Baloney Amputation

Nothing inspires people to malapropism with quite the same intensity as the subject of their own health. It appears an essential human impulse, not merely to mishear one's doctor's diagnosis but to accept it as gospel, however bizarre it may sound, and be positively proud of the challenge it poses to medical science.

'My doctor says I've got acute vagina.'

'It's the old man's disease — my prophylactic gland.'

'They're sending me in next week for my hysterical rectum.'

'I've got to have my aviaries removed.'

'I've had stomach pains for months. The specialist says it could be an ulster.'

James Lees-Milne's diaries record how the American-born London socialite Laura Corrigan astounded her salon with what she presumed a routine piece of medical advice.

'My doctor told me, "If you want to avoid indigestion, you must masturbate, masturbate. . . ."'

A BANANA
A DAY KEEPS
THE DOCTOR
AWAY

'If you want to avoid indigestion . . .'

My Cockney grandmother, back from a visit to her sister in hospital, feelingly described the 'sirloin' drip attached to the patient's arm. It had been difficult to talk, my grandmother said, with all the doctors 'hoovering' around. Nonetheless, she was reassured that her sister seemed to be receiving 'the RIP treatment'.

Barbara Sachs of Rickmansworth recalls that her GP husband was frequently asked by his Cockney patients for a 'stiff ticket' to get off work.

One patient he was examining inquired,
'Tell me, doc — can you really hear anything
through that horoscope?'

Dr Michael Reilly, of Yelverton, Devon,
tells me of the surrealistic surgical enterprises
that can result when hospital typists give
approximate phonetic renderings of the
medical terms dictated to them.

Dr Reilly remembers a report on a Barium
meal X-ray for stomach ulcers which stated —
suitably enough in the West Country — that
the patient's interior revealed 'a phantom
pasty', rather than the faint opacity the
specialist had noticed.

On another occasion, Dr Reilly found

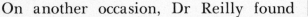

15

himself listed to perform a 'baloney amputation' instead of the below-knee one he had anticipated.

While serving as a corporal in the Royal Army Medical Corps, J. Forrest Penman, of Edinburgh, looked searchingly at a soldier on sick parade and asked what he was complaining of.
'I've got a swelling in my grotto, Corp,' the man replied.

A Washington paediatrician reports that children in her care consciously use malapropisms to make the medical terms they overhear seem less intimidating. The unpleasant bone marrow test for leukaemia has thus become converted into 'the bow and arrow test'. Spinal meningitis is known by the far more companionable name 'Smiling Mighty Jesus'.

A frequent feminine anxiety confided to Dr Alex Sakula, of Reigate, is: 'Doctor, I'm afraid I must be suffering from the mental pause.'

Dr John Trowell, of Sawbridgeworth, Herts, remembers treating a patient who brought with him a diagnosis from the 'Reptile Clinic' (Rectal Clinic).
The diagnosis was 'fissure in ano' — or, as the patient himself rendered it, 'fish in ano'.

A telephone caller to a Gloucestershire hospital baffled the switchboard operator by asking for 'Sir Michael Spears'. It transpired that what she wanted was 'Cervical Smears'.

Jean Prickett of Tenterden, Kent, remembers this sad confidence from a male acquaintance:
'Unfortunately, we can never have children. My wife is inconceivable.'*

In the days of government-issue National Dried milk, a midwife advised that a baby, doing badly with its mother's milk, should be 'put on the Grand National'. Another such prescient soul urged that, to avoid risk of diphtheria, the baby should forthwith be 'humanised'.

A London hospital orderly was sent to the stores for a spiggot to be fitted at the end of a patient's catheter. The storekeeper could make nothing of his statement that Mrs so-and-so's tube needed 'a spinnaker'.

My Washington informant remembers treating a black woman patient who was complaining of menstrual discomfort.
'How's your flow?' the doctor asked.
'Pretty good since I started with that new wax polish,' the patient replied.

C. C. Lindsay of Croydon remembers an old family retainer who went to the doctor

*The male malapropist cause of this problem is 'being impudent'.

complaining of stomach pains, and was much cheered by the diagnosis. 'I've got a slight structure,' she said. 'But it's all right — I shan't have to wear a trestle.'

A Royal Navy doctor's mother proudly tells her friends that her son has now attained the rank of 'Surging Lieutenant Commander'.

The semi-retired senior partner in a Walton-on-Thames medical practice recently heard himself described by one of his patients as 'semi-retarded'.

Worried that a swimmer might get into difficulties off the beach near her house, Brenda Dorley-Brown of Seaview, Isle of Wight, asked her local doctor for some basic instruction in administering 'the Kiss of Death'.

A colleague of Peter Hayes, Gloucestershire County Council's Information Officer, told him she could never use talcum powder because it pored her clogs.

News reaches me of these further alarming medical mishaps and predicaments:

Of a swimmer revived from drowning by 'artificial insemination'.

Of a birth by the painful 'Cistercian' method.

Of a man over 40 experiencing 'a midwife crisis'.

Of a vasectomy patient who wondered if he would ever have 'martial' relations again.

Of the New York woman admitted to an eye hospital for an operation on her 'Cadillacs'.

Of the Florida lady, fearful of childbirth, who, while making love with her husband, obliged him to wear a 'condominium'.

Of a family friend whose doctor tells her she is 'a little obeast'.

Of patients suffering variously from 'teutonic' ulcers, 'malingering' tumours and 'congenial' heart disease.

Of the sane person mistakenly admitted to a 'menthol' hospital.

Of the accident victim who, having severed 'the juggler vein' . . . 'bled like a stuffed pig'.

Of the back sufferer who had lost faith in manipulation by her 'octopus', and — though she feared the needles might hurt — was determined to discover if any relief could be obtained by 'acapulco'.

I hear of horticultural malapropists who proudly exhibit their 'spitoonias', 'enemas' and dahlia 'tumours', and whose great fear, as they nurture their potato crop, is the return of that dread 1950s pest, the 'Corduroy' beetle.

Michael Reilly remembers an old gardener in Plymouth during the World War 2 bombing, who was outraged at the damage done to grassland by 'insanitary' [incendiary] bombs.

Mrs D. Tomlin, of Aylesbury, complimented an elderly gardening neighbour on the wonderful show he had produced. 'Ah —' he said, 'and you know, it's the first time I ever tried growing these here Christian anthems.'

Peter Miln tells me of a postman in Staffordshire, who was much struck by the clematis entwined around the front porch of a house on his route.

'It looks really pretty,' he said to the householder, 'now your wife's got her clitoris to climb all up round there.'

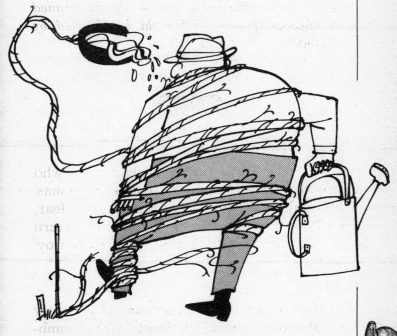

'It looks really pretty now your wife's got her clitoris to climb all up round there . . .'

'Christ the Royal Master leans against the phone . . .'

Childhood's malapropisms stay with one for ever, none more so than those arising from hymns, prayers and the general notion of Heaven, Jesus and God. Who does not remember standing in school assembly, peeping through downcast lashes at the patterns on one's Birthday sandals, resignedly murmuring or singing what the words seemed to be, however strange or even alarming?

A few years ago, a North London teacher asked his class to write down the words of the prayer they had intoned from early infancy at least once a day.

One small boy's written version of 'Our Father Who art in Heaven' was 'Ah far chart eleven. . .' A correspondent from the Portsmouth area tells me he used to pray — quite logically, it seemed — to 'Our Father Who art in Havant'. Another correspondent used to assume that the Being in Heaven was named 'Father Whichart'.

The next line has been interpreted by children since Victorian times as 'Harold be

22

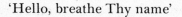

'Hello, breathe Thy name'

Thy name' — or, in the murmurous slur of voices, a cordial but cautious greeting, 'Hello . . . breathe Thy name.' Julia Denison-Smith, from BFPO 15, tells me her small son's version of the line after that was 'Give us this day our day in bed.'

'Lead us not into temptation' assumes new significance among children from London riverside boroughs as 'Lead us not into Thames Station'. J. R. Chester of South Croydon remembers that, when he employed a rather disagreeable German au pair girl, his small son would go on to say, 'But deliver us from Eva.'

23

Philip Brough of Aberdare tells me he used to assume, when his upper class infants teacher said, 'Thine is the Kingdom, the Pa and the Glory', that 'The Pa' was yet another confusing reference to Our Father.

Psalm 23 has always been noted for its striking imagery. 'The Lord is my Shepherd, I shall not want. He maketh me to lie down in green parsley . . . He leadeth me beside distilled waters . . .' And the final, rather worrying reflection: 'Surely Good Mrs Murphy shall follow me all the days of my life . . .'

Hymns have produced such exotic personages as 'Round John Virgin' (featured with mother and child in 'Silent Night'), and the time-honoured 'Gladly, my cross-eyed bear'.

To Mrs M. M. Rotheram, of Guildford, it used to seem no more than prudent that the concluding entreaty of 'Away in a Manger' was 'Stay by my cider till morning is nigh.' A little girl in Elaine Bishop's Totnes Sunday School class used to ask for 'the hymn about the nighties' — 'Now the day is over, nighties drawing near.' Ernest Pratt of West Kirby, Wirral, remembers his four-year-old son's lusty paean to 'All things bright and beautiful, our teachers great and small'. Not to be outdone was Michael Reilly's small niece, in

the chorus of 'Onward Christian Soldiers',
when she sang 'Christ the Royal Master leans
against the phone.'

The Rev. J. H. Davies of Southampton was
told by his mother that she used to think the
Gloria Patri was about a naughty little girl
named Glory — hence 'Glory beat the Father,
ran to the Son, ran to the Holy Ghost.'
Suzanne Beven of Esher remembers always
being rather frightened by references to 'The
Father, The Son and the Holy Ghosty men'.
There is also the story of the small boy,
holding a burial service for a dead bird, who
cheerily intoned: 'In the name of the Father
and of the Son . . . and into the 'ole he goes . . .'

Eric Taylor of Reigate knows a small girl
who firmly believed the opening words of
Handel's *Messiah* were: 'Come for tea, come
for tea my people saith your God . . .'

A Sunday School teacher in Sussex discovered that, when her class repeated The
Creed, most believed that Jesus had suffered,
not under Pontius Pilate but under 'a bunch
of spiders'.

A little boy from Basingstoke, Hampshire,
came home from Sunday School and told his

parents he had been learning about St Paul's conversion on the Domestos Road.

A little girl from Abbots Bromley, Staffordshire, told her mother in great excitement that the prizes at her school speech day were to be presented by 'The Archdemon of Stoke'.

A little boy in Worcestershire thought, with unimpeachable logic, that the Seventh Commandment was 'Thou shalt not come into Dudley.'

As a boy chorister at his local church, R. D. Widdas of South Croydon used to be mystified by the frequent appeals for contributions to 'the Vicar's Tiepin Fund'.

So his youthful ears interpreted 'the Vicar's Stipend Fund'.

The voice of Nat 'King' Cole singing 'Unforgettable' comes back to me from the age of ten or so. The singer's distinctive phrasing seemed to me at one point to spoil the song's mood of unalloyed admiration. I thought he was singing, not 'That's why darling, it's incredible . . .' but *'That's* my darling. It's incredible!' Likewise on Billy Eckstine's 'I Apologise' — bearing in mind my mother's betting proclivities — I thought the line 'If I told a lie . . .' was 'If I totalised . . .'

Modern popular songs, if anything, give greater scope for childish misunderstanding. I hear of a small girl fan of the Three Degrees who skipped round her house singing the refrain 'Bicycle hut' rather than 'My simple heart'; and of another who firmly believed 'Way Down Yonder in New Orleans' to be a song about 'three old ladies with flashing eyes', the notion of Creole ladies being too exotic for her to grasp.

In the Sixties Beat Boom, it was widely believed among children that the chorus to Gerry and the Pacemakers' biggest hit ran: 'You give me a feeling in my heart/like a marrow passing through it'. And that Clarence

'Frogman' Henry's big ballad hit of 1961 was not 'You Always Hurt The One You Love' but 'Your Walrus Hurt The One You Love'.

'I do like it when you smile,' an affectionate little girl told her mother. 'It shows the plimsolls in your cheeks.'

. . . the plimsolls in your cheeks . . .

A little boy in Hull was proud of the fact that whenever Kojak, the TV detective, picked up the phone in his office, he invariably seemed to be saying 'Hello . . . Humberside.'

Kojak was, of course, saying in his brusque New York way, 'Hello . . . Homicide . . .'

A little girl in Newcastle-on-Tyne firmly

28

believed that Elizabeth Taylor lived in Gateshead, rather than Gstaad.

A little girl recently arrived in New York to live told a friend how long she and her mother had had to wait in a department store before the 'alligator' arrived to take them to the fifth floor.

A little boy in Minneapolis was asked by his mother why his friend Brandon never came over to play at his house.

'Brandon can't come here,' the boy replied. 'He's a homosexual.'

On closer examination, he explained he thought a homosexual was someone who only liked being at home.

A little girl in Northamptonshire wrote home from her first boarding school to say that the headmistress had 'calved' at Sunday lunch.

A little boy in Devon said he had not liked to see his mother at the beauty parlour with 'crawlers' in her hair.

A little girl in North London told her teacher that someone had just been to her house to fit the doors and windows with 'giraffe-excluders'.

A little girl of eight had just received a severe scolding from her father, but was determined not to give way to tears. 'That's *it*, Daddy,' she said, scarlet-faced. 'Now I've really taken Uxbridge!'

From school and student essay and examination papers:

'*The three ways of transmitting heat are conduction, conviction and constipation.*'

'*King Henry disguised himself in the garbage of a monk . . .*'

'*This poem begins in medeas rex . . .*'

'*Samson felled a thousand foreskins.*'

Conduction, conviction and constipation . . .

'St Paul was persecuted by the Emperor Nehru.'

'A musket was a most unweedy weapon . . .'

'The practice of having only one wife is called monotony.'

'Socrates died from an overdose of wedlock.'

'Isaac Newton was very studious as a child, when he could often be found embossed in a book.'

'A virgin forest is a place where the hand of man has never set foot.'

'Eugene O'Neill's greatest achievement was winning the Pullet Surprise.'*

*Pulitzer Prize

31

Winning the Pullet Surprise

'*Russia uses the acrylic alphabet.*'

'*At Lord Nelson's funeral, it took 50 sailors to carry the beer.*'

'King George lay in state for two days on a catapult.'

'Pompeii was destroyed by an overflow of red hot saliva.'

'The Equator is a menagerie lion running round the Earth.'

'After the baby butterfly has been a caterpillar, it becomes a syphilis.'

'Salome did the Dance of the Seven Veils in front of Harrods.'

Ned Sherrin tells me of a young actress named Chrissie Kendall who is undisputedly the Mrs Malaprop of the contemporary stage. In Sherrin's hearing recently, she spoke about a friend who had gone off to Israel to live on 'a kebab'. She also habitually refers to the Royal Shakespeare Company as 'the RAC'.

During 1979, her colleagues heard her express mounting concern over 'the ostriches'.

'What ostriches?' a friend inquired.

'The ostriches in prison in Iran,' Ms Kendall replied.

An Appetising Camisole

The lady who attributed her tasty meat dishes
to a plentiful infusion of 'spies and bailiffs' —
spices and bay leaves — made the point well
enough. Good cooks have too much else on
their plates to be bothered with words. And
why should they? Would those 'spies' taste
any the worse for being ground up, as the

same lady said, with a 'pedestal' and mortar? Would a stew not be rather the more appetising for having been simmered at length in an antique 'camisole'? Would one not really prefer to believe in traditional British dishes like 'knockers and mash' or newly popular continental ones like 'camel only'? Only vegetarians could object — and for them there is always the 'mackerel-biotic' diet.

Standbys from the malapropist's store cupboard

Fruit compost
Canine pepper
Desecrated coconut
Tomato catspit
Ogre beans*
Exasperated (or
   paralysed) milk

Wednesday daily
   cheese
Nipplepolitan ice
   cream
Smoky bunion crisps
Peanut bristle

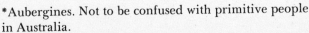

*Aubergines. Not to be confused with primitive people in Australia.

*'She is an excellent cook, clean and good-tempered.
She is leaving us of her own violation.'*
— *Employer's reference, 1930s*

Mary Carter, of Cambridge, remembers a cook who worked for her sister in Gloucestershire and who swore by the old Home & Colonial Stores. When she ran short of something, she would say, 'I'll have to pop out to the Holy Cologne.'

An elderly New York lady refused her granddaughter's cold leek and potato soup with a true Jewish cook's distaste both for its consistency and its outlandish French name.
'No thank you, dear,' she said. 'I don't care for that Vishy-vashy stuff.'

A 'county' mother in Cambridgeshire has been telling friends proudly that her daughter has been accepted for a course at the 'Condom Bleu'.

Sylvia Howard, a chef in Virginia Water, was recently conferring with the supervisor of the hotel cleaning crew.
'If there's any change in the schedule,' the supervisor said, 'I'll be sure to lyonnaise with you.'

The proprietor of a Staffordshire bistro remembers being asked by a customer if wine was served 'by the giraffe'.

The CO of a well-known British regiment is cherished by his junior officers for having once remarked that, what with his love of food and wine and the good things in life, he supposed he was 'a bit of a sodomite'.

A Sloane Ranger and her poorer friend, searching for a cheap place to eat, happened on the Bloomsbury trattoria Mille Pini.

'What about this?' the friend said jocularly. 'A thousand pines.'

'Oh, *no*,' the Sloane Ranger protested. 'It *can't* be as expensive as all that!'

Out on a heavy date, a rash young Londoner asked his companion if she would like to finish their Italian meal with that romantic liqueur which comes in glasses with blue fire licking around the rim.

Calling the waiter, he ordered 'two coffees and two Osso Bucos'.

A haggis-maker named Mr McSween recently confided to the *Meat Trades Journal* that he has 'a gut feeling' that he will soon open his own haggis factory.

The *Sunday Times Magazine* reported in the sixties that when cookery writer Margaret Costa bought a special cut of veal for 'a feast from Valhalla . . . she stuffed it personally with Mr Duckett of Harrods Meat Department.'

The mother of a London advertising man was about to set off for her first ever holiday in Cyprus. 'Whatever you do,' her son counselled, 'you mustn't miss trying the moussaka.'

His mother looked guarded.

'Well, if I don't have any while I'm there,' she said, 'I'll be sure to bring a bottle home.'

A Greek waiter in London extolled the night's special dishes thus: 'I have got stifado and I have got meaty balls.'

Some enticing dishes noted on menus throughout the world

'Stuffed nun'	(*Indian restaurant, Paddington, London*)
'Kidneys of the chef	(*Cathedral restaurant, Granada, Spain*)
'Smoked Solomon'	(*Intercontinental Hotel, Jakarta*)
'Turdy Delight'	(*seafront restaurant, Eilat, Israel*)
'Pig in the family way'	(*available throughout West Germany*)
'Terminal soup'	(*Istanbul airport cafeteria*)

'Steamed dick with vegetables'	*(Chinese restaurant, Gerrard St, London)*
'Quick Lorraine'	*(pub in Ebury St, London)*
'Roast Headlamp'*	*(taverna in Patmos, Greece)*
'Squits with source'	*(restaurant in Gassin, Alpes-Maritimes)*
'Boiled god in parsley'	*(pub in Covent Garden, London)*

*'Head of lamb'

'Calve's dong'	(Hydra Taverna, Athens)
'Fish Rotty and spaghetti Bolograese'	(hotel in North Yemen)
'Battered soul'	(Ashoka Hotel, New Delhi)
'Fried Brian'	(Plat du jour, Geneva, Switzerland)
'Hard-boiled eggs, filled with a delicate curried mouse'	(Bistro blackboard, Manchester)

A Stretcher Named Desire

Staff in the better bookshops tend to become adept at interpreting the bizarre titles for which they are asked by malapropist customers. They know, for instance, that 'Silent Mourner' is the common malaprop version of *Silas Marner*; that 'June the Obscure' will be stocked under H for Hardy; and that anyone seeking 'A Stretcher Named Desire' should be directed to the American drama section.

Valiantly sympathetic sales assistants, both sides of the Atlantic, have unscrambled 'Son of Siriasis' into *The Sun Also Rises*, deduced 'The Fruits of Anger' to mean *The Grapes of Wrath*, and eventually comprehended that 'Freddy The Rabbit Slept Late' was in fact the idiomatic Jewish novel *Friday the Rabbi Slept Late*.

A customer in a Chicago branch of B. Dalton recently caused total bafflement by asking if they stocked 'The Sauce'. Searches of the cookery section, and publishers' catalogues, could find nothing of that name.

What she wanted, it turned out, was Roget's Thesaurus.

Not long afterwards, another customer in the same store asked for Roget's Theodorakis.

Hatchards of Piccadilly tell me that the recent Hamish Hamilton biography *Horrocks: the General Who Led From the Front* was frequently asked for as 'Horrocks: the General Who Fled From the Front'.

A sedate publisher of hobby and handiwork books, some years ago, issued a series under the general title *Making It*. There was *Making It in Pottery; Making It in Fretwork; Making It in Glass . . .*

The publishers could not understand the huge extra sales that accrued to the volume called *Making It in Leather*.

Simon Bainbridge of Hatchards remembers being approached by a downtrodden-looking male customer, who showed him a piece of paper and said, 'My wife's asked me to get this. Do you stock it?'

On the paper was written 'Night Cream by Elizabeth Arden'.

'Remember — the Pope is inflammable . . .'

What survey of word-bungling can be complete without the Rev. Dr. Spooner and his 'piece of cod that passeth all understanding'? This original Spoonerism was, indeed, more malapropism, though Spooner went on to achieve technical perfection with his invocation of the 'Shoving Leopard'. Truth to tell, malapropism has been an essential in English worship since before Henry VIII dissolved the monasteries. Did you know that pubs called The Goat and Compasses were those which originally bore above their entrance the pious words 'God encompasseth us'?

Good News, the magazine of the Additional Curates Society, reports the complaint of an elderly worshipper who was finding it difficult to hear sermons even from the front pew:

'You'll have to come up to date and have microphones, Vicar. The agnostics in this church are very poor.'

The main speaker at a recent Anglican seminar on orthodox theology told his audience of his belief that 'between Man and God there has been placed a vast abbess.'

A churchwarden's wife in the Midlands dramatically described what trouble had been caused in a local house by a poltergeist until the vicar was called in to 'circumcise' it.

A devout Catholic, in theological debate with some Anglican friends, produced the customary clinching argument:
'Ah, but what you must remember is that to us the Pope is inflammable.'

During the 1984 Coal Strike, a London vicar led his congregation in praying for 'reconciliation in the minefields'.

An old age pensioner in North London was continuing to struggle gamely to church, although totally reliant on his Zimmer walking-aid. He assured the vicar he would be quite all right as long as he could use his 'zither'.

From the parish magazine of Little Peover, Cheshire:
'Parishioners will be glad to know that the vicar is recovering well from his unpleasant disposition.'

A future cathedral dean, leading the Litany at an ecumenical gathering, prayed 'that it may please Thee to eliminate all bishops, priests and deacons. . . .'

A parishioner in Co. Durham was reflecting on the irony that so many church buildings had become derelict despite the great wealth accruing to 'the Church Commissionaires'.

'It's as you say every Sunday, Father,' an elderly lady remarked to the Rev. Peter Miln. 'There's nothing but trouble in this transistory life.'

A bride-to-be, overcome by pre-nuptial strain, said she hoped there would be people outside the church, throwing 'spaghetti'.

A church organist in Chicago received a special request from a bride-to-be's mother for a piece of wedding music entitled, so far as she could remember, 'Jesus Walking Through Garfield Park'.
It turned out that she meant 'Jesu Joy of Man's Desiring', by Bach.

A church organist in Kent notified his Parochial Church Council that the 'Larigot' stop on the organ would have to be replaced. He had some trouble subsequently in persuading the PCC that what he needed was not a 'nanny goat'.

From the aviation world, I hear of a jet plane which disturbed a malapropist with its 'Masonic' bangs . . . and of a pilot, forced to leave his aircraft in a hurry by way of the 'ejaculation-seat'.

'Frightened? I was putrified . . .'

The malapropist on heat

'*Well, of all the unmedicated gall . . .*'

'*Now I've really got my gander up . . .*'

'*You nincompimp!*'

'*It's enough to make your head stand on end . . .*'

'*I wouldn't touch him if he were a ten-foot Pole.*'

'*Ha! Hoist by your own leotard!*'

'*He's behaving like a complete cyclepath.*'

'*That's quite enough of your insinnuendoes.*'

'*Angry! I nearly blew my casket!*'

'*Well, that's really put the cap on the pigeon . . .*'

'*I'll have you know I'm not totally illiteral.*'

'*This smells to high herring . . .*'

'*We'll soon nip that idea in the butt.*'

'*What a load of bladderdash!*'

'*Frightened? I was putrified!*'

'*I really thought I'd given up the goat.*'

The Clerk to the Justices in Newcastle-upon-Tyne reports that a witness in his court recently claimed to be in receipt of 'infidelity' benefit.

Divorce cases in British courts frequently turn on the question of 'congenial' rights, or whether a married couple have proved, as they claim, 'totally incombustible'. Petitioners in possession of decrees nisi have many times confirmed that, after six months, they wish their divorces to become 'obsolete'. There was also the co-respondent who, asked to describe his relationship with the defendant wife, assured the judge that it had been 'purely plutonic'.

While covering Cambridge Magistrates Court, I heard a policeman feelingly describe the distress of a woman to whose burgled house he had been called.

'How would you describe her condition when you arrived?' asked Prosecuting Counsel.

'She was in a collapsable state, sir,' the PC replied.

A passionate advocate of rescuing the Falkland Isles from Argentina declared that, after all, Falklanders were 'neuterised British subjects'.

His jingoistic soul was stirred to see the British Task Force sail out of Portsmouth, led by 'HMS Herpes'.

50

'Parlez-vous Francaise un peur?'

British xenophobia has always been best expressed in our attitude to the language of our nearest neighbours. For a thousand years, most Britons have refused to believe that French can mean anything at all unless transliterated to the nearest possible semblance of English. We say 'You can't make a silk purse out of a sow's ear' because our ancestors could not bring themselves to pronounce the French word 'souzière', meaning a cheap cloth scrip. And if the result should be pure gibberish — as when British soldiers in the Great War adapted the Frenchman's classic verbal shrug — well, San Ferry Ann.

The late Kenneth Tynan had an incurable weakness for making French turn phonetic handsprings into English. Tynan it was who rewrote the well-known nursery rhyme to begin 'Un petit d'un petit sat on a wall . . .' and invented the famous French strict tempo orchestra leader 'Charles-Louis d'Ince'.

The whole French attitude of isolationism, Tynan used to say, could be summed up in the pithy gallic maxim 'Pas d'elle yeux rhône que nous'.

Laura Corrigan, the famous Society malapropist of the 1930s, confided to James Lees-Milne how much she was enjoying a biography of 'Richard Gare de Lyon'.

A British ex-serviceman, winner of the Croix de Guerre for heroism, can sometimes be persuaded by his grandchildren to show them what, with typical modesty, he calls 'my Crossed Cigars'.

'Parlez-vous Francaise un peur? Vous comprenez? Good — then you're the missing link this dynamic young sales executive needs. . .'
                    Advertisement in Girl About Town

A friend's mother, speaking of their forthcoming night railway journey through France, volunteered to try to reserve a couple of 'courgettes'.

The Rev Peter Miln is also a noted chef and — thanks to his Belgian ancestry — a fluent French-speaker. At a banquet he attended recently, a Frenchwoman seated on his left began confiding details of the liver trouble to which, like many French people, she is a martyr. Most of the meal was occupied by her harrowing description of this 'crise de foie'.

Towards the end, the Englishwoman seated on Mr Miln's right murmured sympathetically, 'Poor Father — I expect you get awfully tired of hearing about other people's crises of faith.'

The French wife of a *Times* reader always refers to the paper's Portfolio game as 'Profiterole'.

A trendy young Londoner decided to give the family's new French au pair girl a treat by taking her to the weekend market at Camden Lock.

As they passed a stall selling various kinds of savoury pancake, the trendy young Londoner jocularly inquired, 'Do you feel like a crêpe?'

The au pair girl — who had been taught that upper class English people flatten their vowels, and who therefore thought she was being asked 'Do you feel like a crap?' — looked understandably confused.

Travel continues not to broaden the malapropist's mind. However our world may shrink, there will always — one hopes — be travellers in Greece changing their money into 'draculas'; in Spain and Italy visiting the many shrines to 'St Mary Mandolin'; in Switzerland admiring the picturesque alpine 'shillelaghs'; and in Hawaii photographing an authentic 'loo owl'.

I hear from visitors to Saudi Arabia that great kindness and hospitality is shown to

St Mary Mandolin

westerners by the region's 'bed-ridden' tribes-
men. And that in India, even more than
midland Britain, one sees Sikhs with 'turbines'
on their heads, and women attired in colourful
'safaris'.

Disturbing news comes from Alan Crompton
that his mother was swimming in the
Mediterranean when a jellyfish swam up and
wrapped its 'testicles' around her. Apparently,
holidaymakers are reluctant to visit South
America because of the 'toreadors' that have
lately caused such destruction there. More
and more people seem to be trying adventure
holidays in African countries where one can
still go to sleep listening to the sound of native

'tum-tums'. And I am pleased to hear that Bali seems every bit the island paradise it has been painted. A recently returned traveller reports that Balinese sunsets can contain 'all the colours of the rectum'.

Brian Rust, of Pinner, Middlesex, remembers his mother's firm belief that Albanians were people with white hair and pink eyes; that Red Indian war dances took place around a 'talcum' pole; and that, if our leaders did not take care, we might soon be at war with 'Solvent' Russia.

While staying at the Mandarin Hotel, Hong Kong, in 1974, I realised that the next day was my mother's birthday. I telephoned down to the front desk and dictated a greetings telegram, hoping it would reach her Bayswater flat in time.

That evening, a copy of the telegram had been pushed under my door. At the bottom, to my consternation, I saw the word 'Col.'* Surely I had not succumbed to journalistic reflex and sent the message collect. Fearful that my mother might have had to pay for her own telegram from the other side of the world, I telephoned the front desk again. The same Chinese voice as before answered me.

'This is Mr Norman. You sent a telegram to England for me today.'

'Yes.'

56   *in cable-ese, collate — ie, supply copy.

'I want to check something — it wasn't collect, was it?'

'Yes, sir,' the desk-clerk replied indignantly. 'It was *quite* collect!'

During the sixties, a delegation from the British shipbuilding industry paid a visit to several large shipyards in Japan.

'What do you find is your biggest problem?' one delegate asked his Japanese counterpart.

'Our biggest probrem,' the Japanese ship-builder replied, 'is lust.'

The statement was greeted with sympathetic British nods.

A recent visitor to West Germany was clearly affected by that country's strident musical heritage as he described the delay he had experienced while changing trains in Bonn.

'I was stuck for hours,' he lamented. 'All the departure boards were empty and there wasn't a single announcement over the Tannhäuser.'

The incorrigible Laura Corrigan, disembarking from the yacht on which she had been cruising, said it felt wonderful to be on 'terracotta' again.

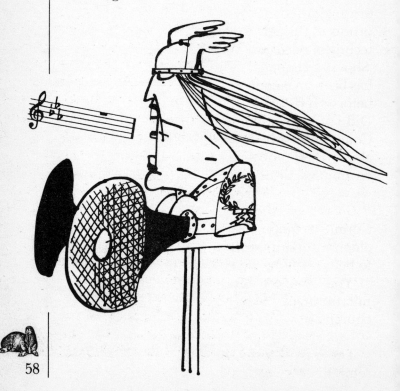

58

A traveller just back from Italy has been telling friends how awe-struck she was on first seeing the Leaning Tower of Pizza.

Richard Burton was once buttonholed in an hotel lobby by an American who claimed intimacy on the strength of also having Welsh forebears.

'You and I ought to get on well, Mr Burton,' he said. 'We're both Selts.'

'No,' Burton replied. 'I am a Selt. *You* are a sunt.'

Tommy Dorsey, the Big Band era's most famous malapropist, once introduced a guest vocalist — of coincidental beefiness — as 'that talented singing steer'. Among Bluesmen, Big Bill Broonzy was noted for his inability to remember any fellow Bluesman's name: he would refer to Scrapper Blackwell as 'Black Scrapwell' and to Fats Waller as 'Fat Wallace'.

All the poignant wisdom of the Blues seems gathered into a remark made by pianist Eubie Blake a few days before his 100th birthday.

'If I'd known I was going to live so long,' he said, 'I'd have taken more care of myself.'*

*He died three days later

A British Rail guard on the Waterloo-Portsmouth service explained over the internal loudspeaker system that the train would be delayed 'owing to a fertility on the line'.

Interesting dogs are owned by malapropists. They include the Cockerel Spanner, the Irish Settler, the Great Dame, the sausage-shaped Datsun and the small — but always game and playful — Shitzy-Witzy.

The Great Dame and the Shitzy-Witzy

'Every morning, he gets this terrible insurrection . . .'

The choicest malapropisms tend to be seasoned with Vim and wax polish and the smell of milk coming to the boil for mid-morning coffee. It is no more than fair to devote a full chapter to the inexhaustible verbal treasury of the British cleaning lady.

'He asked me to marry him twice, but I infused him.'

'I knew it was my coat because it had my entrails in it . . .'

'He drives the motorbike and she sits on the pavilion.'

'I've always been thin. When I was a girl, I was in bed for a year with infantile paraphenalia.'

'I hate injections. That's why I couldn't be a blood doughnut.'

'He's given her a gold singlet ring . . .'

'I couldn't eat any more. I was full to captivity.'

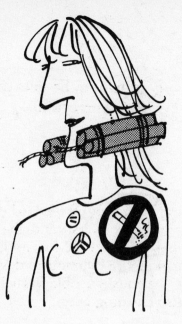

'My daughter's bought a lovely new pair of dynamite earrings.'

'She's on this terrible diet — she's getting really emancipated.'

'He wore his uniform for a long time after the War. You see, he couldn't afford a new set of privvies.'

'She asked me if I liked the new colour scheme in her kitchen. I said "I'm not enamelled of it . . ."'

'She's changed her name you know. She done it by Interpol.'

63

'*These Russians are always defecating, aren't they?*'

'*— he was walking round, starch naked.*'

'*Beautiful skin she's got. Just like allyblaster.*'

M. Richards, of London SW1, had ordered a wine rack from the Army and Navy Stores. A note from his cleaning lady said: 'The Army and Navy phoned. Your wild rat has arrived.'

C. C. Lindsay, of Croydon, remembers an arch-practitioner named Mercy, who announced she was giving her nephew a 'manicure set' for his birthday. Closer investigation revealed that she meant a Meccano set.

Employing a rare anagrammatic talent, Mercy said she knew a certain neighbour was back from holiday, having seen her in 'the telephone eskimo'.

For some years, Agnes Rodgers of Melton Mowbray organised an annual 'Alfresco Fete', which her cleaning lady always referred to as 'Your frisky feetie'.

The cleaning lady came in one day to report that her daughter had been taken to the opera by a highbrow boyfriend.

'Which opera?' Mrs Rodgers asked.

'Hyena,' the cleaning lady replied.

'I gave her her train fare,' a Stafford cleaning lady reported about her granddaughter's journey south. 'I didn't want her highjacking her way up and down that motorway.'

A South London cleaning lady was confiding in her employer about the 'demands' still made on her by her 70-year-old husband.

'Every morning when he wakes up,' she said, 'he's always got this terrible insurrection.'

'It's a doggy dog world . . .'

Gems of malapropist philosophy

'A woman's place is in a home'

'No man is in Ireland'

*'It's a doggy dog world'**

'We pass like chips in the night'

'I'd say it was a vicious circus'

'Never give up. Keep looking for the bluebeard'

'All that's just a splash in the pan'

'Life isn't all beer and kittens'

'I'll just chuck it up to experience'

*Dog eat dog

During his recent Thames Television series, London hairdresser Trevor Sorbie demonstrated a spiky new cut on a girl model of already advanced punkishness.

As he began snipping, he explained that the idea was to make the final look 'as deranged as possible'.

During the 1983 Libyan Embassy siege, a local office worker told a colleague it would be impossible to get to work because police were throwing 'an accordion' around St James's Square.

While working as a probation officer in Derby, Eric Wall encountered a young delinquent's parents who admitted they were not married, but said they had been 'happily co-rabbiting for years'.

A friend of actor and Soho-dweller Richard Huggett was enthusing about the recent great improvement in Leicester Square.

'It's so much better,' he said, 'now that it's become a pederastrian precinct.'

Prawns in the Game

Brian London, that lachrymose British heavy-weight, summed up the predicament of many a modern sports personality when he gazed at his interviewer, as emotionally as a British heavyweight could gaze, and remarked, 'I'm just a prawn in the game.' Pinioned by TV lights, chivvied by microphones to explain the inexplicable — generally at moments of high physical stress — who among us would not tumble into the same communal bath of gibberish? It is as unfair to mock sports commentators for howlers committed under the strain of perpetual improvisation. It is quite unfair: still, we shall go ahead with it.

When Beau Jack, the American fighter, fell on hard times, he would beg his former promoters to give him any match, even without prize money, 'just to relieve the monopoly'.

Ivor Powell, the Welsh manager of Port Vale F.C., used to attribute his team's good results to 'the harmonium in the dressing-room'. At moments of mid-match excitement, he was heard to shout at his forwards: 'I've told you lads a hundred times! Veer *straight*!'

Commentating on the pursuit cycling event at the 1976 Montreal Olympics, the BBC's David Sanders observed: 'The East Germans are knitting well.'

Asked to comment on a disastrous game for his Philadelphia Phillies football team, coach Danny Ozark replied, 'Even Napoleon had his Watergate.'

A sports news reader on Radio Luxembourg recently referred to 'former Olympic swimming star Dunce Goodhew'.

Jimmy Hill, the BBC's egregious football presenter, is fond of saying he has just been 'incommunicado' with this or that match correspondent over the studio telephone.

Alan Weeks, the athletics commentator, has been heard to enthuse about 'Marie Scott from Fleetwood, the 17-year-old who's really plummeted to the top . . .'

Ex-racing champion Jackie Stewart remarked of a certain Grand Prix: 'There's enough Ferraris there to eat a plate of spaghetti.'

Ken Barrington, the former England batsman, carried the art of malapropism from the crease into management. 'Pitch it up more,'

he once instructed a bowler when coaching the England Test team. 'You've got to catch the batsman in two man's land . . .'

Describing his own black, bushy hair, Barrington once said it was 'like a grenadier's fuzzby'. He would also recall that, though some of his early Test tours had been 'quite inoculous', others had been organised as badly as 'Gymkhana's [Fred Karno's] Army'.

His most dramatic story was of witnessing a riot in Bangalore when, he said, the police 'infiltrated the crowd with a couple of hundred plain clothes protectives.'

Commentating from Israel, the BBC's David Vine observed: 'Today, the Holy Land is a Mecca for tourists . . .'

'Once again, it was the swimming pool that set the crowd alight.'

Radio 2 Olympic report, 1980

'In a moment, we hope to see the pole vault over the Satellite . . .'

David Coleman at the Montreal Olympics

'Now Juantareno opens his legs — and really shows his class. . . .'

Ditto

On television last season, American football coach Bill Peterson, admitted that a disappointing game by his team, the Houston Oilers, had left him 'utterly chestfallen'.

However, he thought he had found the 'crutch' of the problem and from here on would be trying an entirely new 'floormat'.

He added that the Oilers were being urged to dismiss every thought from their minds save that of reaching the Superbowl championship.

'I'm telling them, "Night and day, you guys should be thinking just one thing . . . *Sugar bowl*!"'

A recent TV documentary about vandalism focused on the plight of an old man living alone and neglected in one room in one of the worst affected areas. The old man was, however, tough, self-reliant and devoid of self-pity. He could stand his poor conditions, he told his interviewer — what depressed him were 'the evangelists who come round at night, smashing windows and kicking in the doors.'

Miss A. Chapman, of Forest Gate, London, tells me how fond her mother used to be of that fine English oratorio 'The Dream of Geronimo'.

John Parker remembers how impressed one of his most distinguished York University colleagues was by the first volume of Lord

Clark's autobiography — in particular, the chapters dealing with Clark's Edwardian idle-rich father.

'He never did a day's work after he was twenty,' Mr Parker's colleague reported. 'He bought a whole series of yachts, owned an hotel in France — he even broke the bank at Monte Cassino.'

An elderly aunt of Peter Ustinov came from Russia to Britain during the crisis days of World War II. Travelling by train during the blackout, she was perplexed to find all the station name-boards obliterated. Time and again, as her train flashed through, the only word that could be distinguished on a darkened platform was the ghostly legend 'Gentlemen'.

Arriving at her destination, the short-sighted old lady asked why so many different places in Britain were all called 'Cheltenham'.

'You can't have your pound of flesh and eat it too . . .'

Malapropists in the Media

The crimes against language perpetrated daily by newspapers, radio and television seldom include anything so harmless and amusing as a malapropism. Witless clichés, inane mixed metaphors and other consequences of striving for effect without thought, in general leave us as insensible to the words as are their users. We should be all the more grateful for these occasional blunders into vividness.

'Astronaut Alan Shepard is just beginning the final run through of his chick-list . . .'
ABC-TV commentary, Apollo Moon landing, 1972

'Tonight's orchestral concert comes to you from the Bath Room at Pump . . .'
BBC Third Programme, 1950s

'A new film by Jacques Cousteau, the famous French underwear explorer . . .'
Channel 13 TV, New York

74   William Deedes, editor of the *Daily Telegraph*,

Jacques Cousteau, the French underwear explorer

is cherished by Fleet Street, not only for his way of pronouncing 'shome mishtake', but also for what his staff called Deedesisms — a mixture of malapropism and mixed metaphor brought on by the great man's besetting vagueness. When a *Telegraph* reporter left the paper to join a magazine, Deedes shook his hand warmly and said, 'Goodbye my dear chap. Remember — don't burn your boots.'

Deedesisms can enliven the *Telegraph*'s political line, as when the editor remarked to a leader-writer, 'That Peter Carrington, you know, still weighs a lot of ice . . .' On the trials of editorship, Deedes has been heard to observe variously that 'You've got to keep all your feathers in the air', 'You can't make an omelette without frying eggs' and, most runically, 'You can't have your pound of flesh and eat it too.'

'Don't go away, folks. After the break, we'll have a wildlife expert here, and he's going to show us a horny owl . . .'
Johnny Carson on The Johnny Carson Show

The *County Express*, Stourbridge, recently reported a talk on smocking and rugs at Wordsley Community Centre as 'a talk on smoking drugs'.

During World War II, the exiled King Carol of Romania agreed to broadcast over the BBC from London to sustain the morale of his subjects under Nazi rule.

The poignant drama of the occasion was somewhat spoiled by the unsuitably merry sound which broke out on the air immediately before the king began to speak. The BBC Sound-Effects department had been asked to provide a fanfare. But the sound-effects man's cue had been accidentally mistyped as 'funfair'.

Some novel musical celebrities currently being mentioned by radio disc jockeys in Britain and America:

    John Lemon
    Mick Jaeger
    Daisy Doris
    Cher Porno
    Elephants Gerald*
    Gladys Knight and the Pimps

A commentator on American public radio recently cast his listeners' minds back to the 1972 'Watergate bake-in' and went on to recall how former President Richard Nixon had escaped impeachment by 'a hare's breath'.

Wedding reports in local newspapers are usually written with the aid of forms filled up by the couples themselves, or their parents.

*Ella Fitzgerald

Mick Jaeger

As a junior reporter on the *Hunts Post*, I transcribed many accounts of services in which brides went to the altar carrying 'bunches of Friesians', and organists very often played that well-loved nuptial hymn 'Love's Divine'. A

certain bridal going-away outfit I shall always remember was detailed on the form as 'a lemon two-piece with a stone hat and matching accessories'. There was also the wedding gift of an elderly bridegroom to his rather

younger bride which a misplaced comma
rendered, no doubt all too accurately, as 'an
antique, pendant'.

An evening paper in the Midlands, some
years ago, had to report the remarriage of its
own managing director on the same Saturday
as the start of the football season and the
consequent reappearance, that same evening,
of the football results edition popularly called
The Sporting Pink, or Pink 'Un.

In the centre of the front page, the
managing director was pictured with his
mature bride outside the city Register Office.
Next to their photograph appeared the
jubilant announcement:

HURRAH! HURRAH! HURRAH!
The Pink 'Un Comes Out Again Tonight

*A statement was issued last night by the British
Broadcorping Castration . . .'*
BBC Home Service, 1950s

The old-fashioned American police reporter
was hired for his toughness and his ability to
get on with both cops and hoodlums rather
than his education or the elegance of his prose.
Walter Head, of the old New York *Herald-
Tribune*, recalls one such correspondent on
the phone from the scene of a crime to his
rewrite man, dictating:

'The cop fired. The bullet whickershammed
off the wall and struck the corpse in the

cadaver . . .'

Mr Head writes to me also of a suicide case when the police would allow only one reporter of the dozen-odd present to view the death scene.

As the nominee came downstairs again, his colleagues gathered round to hear the grisly details.

'Gentlemen,' he began impressively, 'the corp was dressed in . . .'

'You mean corpse don't you, John?' someone interrupted.

'There was only one for Chrissake,' John replied impatiently.

A Norfolk weekly paper published a fulsome obituary tribute to a woman famous for the flower arrangements she had provided at all the district's major social occasions.

'It will not be the same winter season without Mrs —,' the obituary said, 'and some of the most important balls in the county are going to miss her special touch.'

'At 8.50 tonight, we shall be broadcasting Haydn's Cremation . . .'

BBC Radio 3

Johnny Carson: 'We have Jack Nicholson on the show later.'

Charo (exotic Latin actress): 'Oh, I just love his movies.'

Carson: 'Did you see the one about the sanitarium?'

Charo: 'Oh yes — One Flew Over the Cuckoo's Nuts . . .'

Ray Seaton, of Wombourne, Staffs, reminds me of the colourful mistakes sometimes make by typists who take down journalists' copy over the telephone. As a reporter on the old Leicester *Evening Mail*, he once 'phoned in' the report of a public meeting where reference had been made to Pandit Nehru. It was taken down by the copytypist and printed as 'Bandit Nehru'.

A news bulletin in French on the BBC World Service included an item about population levels in the Cape region of South Africa. Impelled by Spooner's ghost, the announcer referred at one point to 'La copulation immense du Pape'.

The source of most inadvertent filth in newspapers was the tendency of the old Linotype machine to substitute the letter i for o or a. Thus many a famous footballer was said to have 'sent a magnificent long shit over the bar'. Thus *The Times*'s famous reference to Queen Victoria's opening of the Forth Bridge, when it stated that 'The Queen herself graciously pissed over the magnificent edifice.'

The worst such substitution I ever knew — a rogue example — happened on the *Hunts Post* in a story I had written about a female youth leader's visit to Huntingdon on an exchange scheme, and the official lunch which had marked her departure.

The copy I wrote said 'At the conclusion of the lunch, Molly thanked all the Borough Councillors who had taken part in the scheme.' It appeared in the *Hunts Post* as 'At the conclusion of the lunch, Molly whanked all the Borough Councillors who had taken part in the scheme.'

'*The girl has been flown to America for treatment of a spinal tuna . . .*'

BBC Radio 4 News

At the end of the sixties there was a staff purge on one of the leading Sunday colour supplements. Among the casualties was an executive who had previously dominated the magazine with grittily sentimental stories about working class life in his native Tyneside. The new editor was an old Etonian with a classical education and no empathy whatever with pit heaps or whippets.

Over a pub lunch during the transition, the Tynesider spoke wistfully about an issue of the magazine he had always dreamed of organising — a 'theme' issue that would have summed up his whole view of journalism in the modern world. The pub was noisy, and it seemed to the new editor that his companion was repeatedly stating a portentous, though obscure Latin axiom: 'Non Sequiris Vox'.

He was in fact observing — as his journalistic masterpiece would have been headlined — 'There's none so queer as folks'.

From the commercial and clerical world, I hear of a company whose personnel manager is currently offering new employees substantial 'French benefits' . . . of a factory owner humanely trying to reduce staff by a process of 'nutrition' . . . of economic calculations being made for the next 'physical' year, and current correspondence kept in a 'pretending' file . . . of a particularly reliable clerical worker whose office manager told her not to consult him on every small matter, but wherever possible to use her own 'discrepancy'.

The richest clerical malapropisms tend to occur when Pitman's shorthand — a system of phonetic symbols — has to be transcribed by someone unwilling to perform the additional job of thinking. Hence, in a Hereford solicitor's office, the term 'res judicata' could be rendered by an indifferent typist from her shorthand as 'raise Judy Carter'. Hence, a half-witted temp doing invoices in an Oxford office could convert 'sum accrued due' unflinchingly into 'some crude Jew'. Hence, the unconscious pragmatism of a temp in a City of London merchant bank when she transcribed the dry words 'triennial balance-sheet' into the far more sporting 'try any old balance-sheet'.

Efficiency is, of course, not always accompanied by verbal alertness. A highly efficient PA, seeing that the boardroom tape recorder was malfunctioning just before an important directors' meeting, gallantly took down the complex proceedings in shorthand. Arriving late for lunch with a colleague, she explained she had been delayed by doing 'a hand job' for the directors.

'It's your name we're paying for, Mr Bloomfield . . .'

Demonstrating that malapropists are generally as deaf to names as to words — and that few *faux pas* are more galling to the recipient — we reprise our international cast of Goldwyn, Lennon, Kendall et al.

Leo Abse MP was being introduced to a meeting in his Welsh constituency by a chairman who, time and again, referred to him as 'Mr Abbs'.

Unable to stand it any longer, the MP leaned forward, twitched the speaker's coat-tail and whispered:

'Call me Abs-*ey*.'

'All right,' the gratified chairman whispered back. 'And you can call me Jonesey.'

In the 1930s, Samuel Goldwyn paid a huge sum to lure the best-selling novelist Louis Bromfield on to his payroll as a scriptwriter at MGM. Bromfield was assigned an office and a secretary — and then forgotten. Six months after arriving, he still had not been given a picture to write.

At length he went to Goldwyn and said his conscience would not allow him to accept so much money for doing nothing.

Goldwyn got up from his desk and slipped an arm kindly round Bromfield's shoulders.

'You don't understand,' he said. 'It's your name we're paying for, Mr Bloomfield.'

The architect Sir Edward Maufe arrived late for a formal banquet, but tried to make his entrance as discreet as possible. Approaching the president of the top table, he murmured, 'I'm Maufe.'

'But my dear chap,' the president demurred, 'you've only just got here.'

A secretary at Corgi Books recently put through a call from Jonathan Cape executive Ahna Stamatiou, informing her boss 'It's our Mr Matthews . . .'

While playing for George VI and his family at Windsor Castle in the 1940s, Louis Armstrong dedicated a number to the King with the words: 'Dis next one's for you, Rex.'

The American pop journalist Tony Scaduto, in his book about Mick Jagger's trial and imprisonment for drug possession in 1967, referred to the then editor of *The Times* as 'William Rees-Moog'.

When John Lennon met Harold Wilson in 1964, it was in the star-struck Wilson's capacity as 'honorary barker' of the Variety Club of Great Britain.

Lennon, being violently hung over, was even more fuzzy about names than usual. Hearing Mr Wilson described as a barker — and remembering Britain's famous butterscotch manufacturer — he addressed the future prime minister throughout the function as 'Mr Dobson'.

During the days of cinema newsreels, one member of each camera crew was responsible for filling out the 'dope sheet' with information to be written into the commentary.

In the Ascot Royal enclosure, a 'dope sheet' man from Gaumont-British News approached a Society beauty whose hat had just been filmed — the Hon Mrs Watt-Piper.

'Can I have your name, please Ma'am?' he said.

'Watt-Piper,' the Society beauty replied, smiling brightly.

'None of 'em,' the man retorted with loyal pride. 'I work for Gaumont-British News.'

The Detroit radio commentator Hal Youngblood tells a feeling tale of going to interview Sir Clifford Curzon about the latter's forthcoming piano recital with the Detroit Symphony Orchestra. In the course of an hour, Youngblood found himself being variously addressed by Sir Clifford as 'Mr

Redpath,' 'Mr Wheelwright', 'Mr Greengrocer', 'Mr Goodpasture', and 'Mr Blackpool'.

At last, the interviewer gently pointed out that his name was, in fact, Hal Youngblood.

'Ah yes, of course. Forgive me,' Sir Clifford replied. 'When you get to my age, the memory's the first thing to go, Mr Shuttlethwaite . . .'

Bidding farewell to Sir Samuel Hoare, after the British Foreign Secretary had visited MGM, Samuel Goldwyn added: 'Please give my best wishes to Lady W.'

Chrissie Kendall, the National Theatre's budding young Mrs Malaprop, has been heard to express deep admiration for the acting skill of 'Joan Playwright'. Ms Kendall's own agility at doing back-somersaults has sometimes led her to compare herself with 'Tallulah Handbag' (or even 'Tallulah Bunkbed').

While at drama school, she was advised to read Stanislavsky. She asked her friend Annette how the name was spelt.

'S.T.A.N. . .' Annette began.

'Oh, I know how to spell his *first* name,' Ms Kendall said with dignity.

The Swedish explorer Thor Heyerdahl had been filming late at BBC Television Centre and was waiting in the main lobby for a radio cab. After long delay, a cab drew up outside. The driver walked in, looked round, ignored

Thor Heyerdahl and sat down on a bench.

'Excuse me,' the explorer ventured. 'I think I'm the one you're waiting for.'

'Not me, mate,' the driver said. 'I was told to come and pick up four Airedales.'